SAGITTARIUS HOROSCOPE 2020

Sagittarius Horoscope

2020

Copyright © 2019 Mystic Cat

All rights reserved. This book or any portion thereof may not be reproduced or used in any manner whatsoever without the express written permission of the publisher except for the use of brief quotations in a book review.

The information accessible from this book is for informational purposes only. None of the data within should be regarded as a promise of benefits, a claim of cures, a statutory warranty, or a guarantee of results to be achieved.

The images are used under license from Shutterstock, Dreamstime, or Deposit-photos.

Sagittarius

Sagittarius Dates: November 22 to December 21
Symbol: Archer
Element: Fire
Planet: Jupiter
House: Ninth
Colors: Maroon, navy blue

JANUARY HOROSCOPE

ASTROLOGICAL & ZODIAC ENERGY

INNOVATIVE ~ EXPRESSIVE ~ VISIONARY

WORK & CAREER

This is a time which delivers essential news. It may have you feeling unsettled, a restless and spontaneous chapter encourages you to create change. Shifting sands can feel unstable, yet there is so much fun to be had, you can enjoy the change of pace. It's a time of learning a new area and growing your life, this takes you to an original path. Looking at the past provides you with valuable insight, you can see how your life has transformed over time, and it does draw clarity which enables you to feel comfortable about finishing up this chapter of life, and moving towards a new area soon. It is a time of important creativity. There is something ahead you have been waiting for. As you approach this destination, you may feel more nervous than excited. It does initiate change, and this can feel difficult. Taking time to build foundations, does keep you grounded when life becomes a whirlwind of excitement. A surprise arrives which offers you a remarkable chapter of self-discovery. Various elements are coexisting in your life, each aspect affects a different perspective, this is intimately interconnected, maintaining balance does place you in the ideal position to see expansion occurring on all levels. It aligns you beautifully towards a breakthrough, this is a lucky break, it recognizes you becoming involved in launching an area which inspires and interests you. It is a fantastic time to expand your horizons. Harnessing the energy of fire, Sagittarius makes essential progress. The Friday the 10th Full moon in Cancer coincides with a lunar eclipse also in Cancer. This brings a strong emotional element into your life, it has you tapping into a deeper awareness around your working goals. It the critical month for plotting the course ahead, you plant the seedlings of aspirations, which blossom over the coming months. The lunar New Year occurs on the 25th of January, this is the Chinese year of the Rat, an auspicious year which offers you plenty of luck and good fortune in 2020.

LOVE & ROMANCE

Good things come to those single Sagitarrians who wait, a superb opportunity to deepen a situation is coming into your life. It puts a strong emphasis on developing a bond which brings joy into your life. It is a time which twinkles with potential, you have been on the longest of journeys, and discovering a compatible partner leaves you feeling amazingly happy. It is a remarkable time which heightens your romantic potential. You may find someone is attentive this month, they capture your interest and have you excited about the potential possible. It does open the gates towards a happy chapter. You feel there is a remarkable bond, it develops through the sharing of experiences. Together, you attend fun and exciting social events. Being with your friends creates a relaxing ambient environment to better get to know this person. You enjoy the chance to circulate with this charismatic character. Meeting this person draws a new direction for you, it brings your personal life to a new phase, it is a time which is grounded, practical, and contains energy which carries you forward towards the attainment of long term plans. This is a person who takes notice of you, they shower their attention on the situation, and place a strong emphasis on getting to know you better, it lets you explore the potential for a heartfelt adventure with them.

The Sagitarrius in a relationship find that this relationship is one which requires maintenance, it does flourish under a banner of new potential, this occurs with the Friday the 10th Full moon in Cancer which coincides with a lunar eclipse also in Cancer. This brings a strong emotional element into your life and opens hidden pathways towards more in-depth and more open communication. Soon, this opens the doors to a new portal, life changes, progression picks up as things shift forward. It does draw you towards a happier chapter. It is a bond which benefits from open communication and having the kind of conversations which explore more buried feelings. This is a person who brings out your charms and does feel inspired to be with you. You resolve the blocks which hold you back. There is no other option if you are to reveal this true potential. Broadening your perception helps you plan your future course, it brings you to a time where you worry less about the past and more about your future goals and dreams. It brings new joy into your world, and you move forward, gracefully with the one you chooses to share their life experiences with you.

IDEAS & CREATIVITY

All in all, you are in a time of change, it does take you to a very positive phase, it brings new options to challenge your mind. You accomplish much by having an open heart and being willing to better your circumstances. You may become increasingly focused on improving your home life, and can transform your situation towards the achievement of a long-held dream. This is certainly possible, being proactive, helps clear the path forward. You discover life supports your goals when an offer crosses your way, it encourages you to shift your focus forward. It comes into your life as a big plus, giving you the energy and drive to create a stellar outcome. An area which is seen as a daunting limitation is resolved, it heightens your confidence and has you moving ahead towards obtaining your plans with a sense of assertiveness. Acting on, your instincts produce results. You are doing fantastic work in the world, it does draw you towards a substantial phase of growth, a swirl of new activities arrive to expand your mind and tempt you towards creative expression. It is a time of ideas, and some profound insights may bring forth a new venture to develop. Your analytical mind is a powerhouse of potential. In true style, you ground your ideas in a new area, it embodies the essence of drawing happiness into your life. Remaining open to new learning does bring expansive energy to light, it crosses your path with a visionary aspect, it reclaims your creativity and yields terrific results. You are rewarded for the challenges that you have navigated and overcome. It sees an exceptional chapter arrive, which stages several positive events in quick succession. It is time which draws a balance between your practical life and your need for spiritual growth. It offers you an opportunity to release blocks, you are not restrained by the past and can experience pure light and well-being. This energy arrives like a breath of fresh air, it sees you feeling inspired and brings forth your best qualities. You are proactive and curious about life, your strength is on the rise, leading the way forward.

ISSUES & HURDLES

Sagittarius is used to forward motion. But the Full Buck Moon in Cancer, Luna eclipse combo urges you to slow down, create space to heal, and reflect on life's changes and the larger cycle you are in. The past is a time of wisdom and learning, it has been a worthy phase of emotional growth. This trip down memory lane occurs as a form of synchronicity. It is guiding you towards healing and closure, it helps you shut the door on an outworn area, and you know instinctively that this is the correct course. It is a time of healing. A new portal of life will open for you, change is arriving to shift your focus towards a happier chapter. It's a time where you reach a crossroads, decisive action is needed to cross the line in the sand and head towards a direction which is in alignment with your spirit. It does show you can make the choices necessary to follow your heart. Your intuition is guiding you, you are highly intuitive at this time, able to recognize signs, and understand there is a more profound calling tempting you're towards growth. Your spirit animal this month is a tiger, resilient and fierce. You protect areas which you feel passionate about. It does see you being someone who explores the highs and depths of human emotions, seeking challenges, you love to test your capabilities. Your tiger side is fast-paced, resilient, and tenacious. You hunt out new options which provide you with a scintillating path towards success. You can call upon tiger to offer you protection and guidance. There is travel on the horizon for you, this relates to deepening a personal situation. You discover an area is calling your name, and it is taking you out of your comfort zone, but the results are worthwhile. It is an intense phase of following your heart and moving in alignment with your intuition. This expands your vision of what is possible for you this Chinese year of the Rat, which begins on the 25th of January.

FEBRUARY HOROSCOPE

ASTROLOGICAL THEME & ZODIAC ENERGY

INSPIRED ~ LIVELY ~ ROUSING

WORK & CAREER

The beginning of February is a time of steady progress for Sagittarius in the workplace. Some gains are made, this gives you a strong indication of what can be achieved throughout this year. The first Supermoon for 2020 occurs in your sign on February 9th. You enter a time of finding balance during this lunar phase, if things have felt uncertain recently, you get a better knowledge of the direction ahead through quiet contemplation. Having faith in the path forward sees you moving more consciously and confidently towards an area which offers stability and long term gain. News arrives to inspire you towards change, your creativity is heightened to facilitate a merger which elevates your situation. Life is an adventure, expanding your horizons broadens your experience, it guides you towards an area which gives you room to grow your talents. Your gifts are rising. This brings a plethora of opportunity to tempt you towards growth. This is a time of change, life is set to become better, more expansive, and this sees news arrive. However, in the second half of February, progress may slow to a snail's pace when Mercury retrograde begins on Tuesday the 18th. This is going to put a spanner in the works which disrupt your flow of productivity. It does create an environment where you may have to step backward to reintegrate this problematic energy into your working environment. Additionally, the new moon in Aquarius on the 23rd brings curious news into your working life. This information brings with it rejuvenating energy to help stabilize you over the Mercury retrograde phase.

LOVE & ROMANCE

Singles discover a secret arrives mid-month when someone shares a big reveal. A revelation occurs when a friend shares a secret with you soon. This is news, it does provide you with insight into a situation which offers you potential, this is a golden nugget where you can advance a goal, it is a fortunate time, being in close talks with this person gives you a new view of possibilities. It does provide valuable support and builds foundations around your home life. A lovely perk coming into your life soon. This is a windfall opportunity, it gives you an option to grow your situation, and you may even decide to branch out into a new area. Life supports your expansion, negotiating the path ahead does see you embrace the spirit of optimism, it favors an active phase of growth which draws heightened security. A shift forward does position you towards advancing a dream. This is something completely different, it lets you take full advantage of an opportunity which opens. It is a time of improvement around your home life, a gathering with friends sets the scene for a lovely phase of harmony. It is a time of happy news, and a celebration ahead draws joy into your world. It is a busy time which focuses on achieving long sought after goals.

The Sagitarrius in a relationship finds that their partner's commitment to the situation is blossoming. Exciting changes are going on around your life, this enables you to make progress towards feeling more secure and comfortable, it does bring advancement into your home life. You are reaching an elevation of potential in the area of romance, that's wonderful, it brings you an opportunity to deepen this situation, it draws a time which sees more shared responsibilities, and it does indicate the sharing of experiences which see you proactively involved in developing this situation. A lucky break is coming, good fortune paves the way for a harmonious union to unfold. Having faith in the outcome is going to pay dividends, and a long-awaited dream is possible. As you move forward, news arrives, which enables you to raise the bar of your dreams. It shifts your focus forward and releases you from delays and frustrating conditions which have prevented you from reaching your goals. A sign arrives to guide you forward, it culminates in the achievement of an important endeavor. You are going to light up new options based around your home situation. This culminates in an impressive outcome, it does see you achieving a goal which brings joy into your life. Seeing your home sector improving is a fantastic boost, it gives you the confidence to plan larger goals, it gives you a chance to dream and plan for future growth. A gateway opens, a shift forwards is possible.

IDEAS & CREATIVITY

During the February 9th Supermoon in Leo, you unwrap a cycle of new creative energy. Focusing on self-development does open your world to new opportunities. It moves your focus forward, it creates a very potent shift, as it does bring creativity and new ideas into your world. This is a refreshing time, and it seems certain adjustments being made to harmonize and draw balance. These signs can feel subtle but contain hidden power, as it guides you gently towards new levels of potential. This is the beginning of a new chapter, insight, and inspiration pave the way forward. Ideas are flowing into your life which helps spark a new chapter potential. You may find yourself guided towards an area which holds promise, innovative stirrings are heightening your creative abilities. This enables solutions to be found, it provides you with ample room to grow a dream. Being flexible, broadening your perception gives you a broader landscape. It shifts your creativity into high gear, you see solutions, and discover a new path is open. You are ready to spark a new journey, this is highly creative, it's currently evolving, so what you view as possible today is likely to change to a broader view tomorrow. It does inspire and delight, providing you with a trailblazing chapter of potential.

There is an impressive total of 4 supermoons in 2020. The more you tune into it, the more you are aware that you are going in the right direction. Your epiphanies are dynamic and radical, your innovate ideas blossom under these supermoons.

Issues & Hurdles

You are completing a cycle, life has been draining and demanding. This is set to change. As you move forward, you draw powerful energy into your life which helps release the pressure, in the end, you discover that you can resolve things to your benefit. It does bring your situation to a happy conclusion, regardless of hurdles, what counts the most, is your ability to rise above any obstacles and ultimately succeed. You have the strength to see this through to its final conclusion, wiping the slate does create space for new potential. You have this in the bag, you know the direction you are headed towards, that is in your favor. Making a firm decision, you draw a line in the sand, there's no going back for you. You are ready to release outworn energy, heal the past, and begin a new chapter towards the realization of your dreams. It is a time where you can focus on improving your home situation. If you have found there was friction in your life, this is set to change. Feeling unsettled or restless is a signpost, it's guiding you to create a shift which draws more abundance into your life. Small changes can add up to substantial benefits, making those necessary essential moves, provides you with a cornucopia of new opportunities. There are lovely indications that see the fulfillment of a dream arriving in your life soon. It does release the issues which have held your progress back. All systems point to a happier chapter ahead for you. It has been a time where you may have felt yourself struggling, many problems created a weight on your shoulders. Streamlining and understanding the right direction helps move a new flow of energy into your life.

Mercury retrograde this month can bring your energy down as well. Create a space to honor this chapter, and know that it too will pass in a few weeks, bringing with it a new flow of potential., be aware that this energy does crop up several times a year, and you can adjust by maintaining a broader perception of why this is happening, and know that you can wait it out. Keeping a flexible outlook helps you when Mercury Retrogrades appearance mid-month, this difficult energy is going to soon make way for smoother waters in March.

MARCH HOROSCOPE

ASTROLOGICAL THEME & ZODIAC ENERGY

PERSISTENT ~ CONSTRUCTIVE ~ DRIVING

WORK & CAREER

Slow and steady wins the race at work this March. The Full Moon in Virgo is another supermoon. As the season changes, so do your situation. New energy arrives to offer room to grow your options. It is a time of abundance and magic, this opens a new book of potential. It does harness the energy of manifestation, a strong theme of advancement is currently running through your life. It does pave the way forward towards a soul-stirring chapter which encourages you to dive into uncharted territory. Change is in the air, a fresh wind of potential arrives to bring gifts of stability and security. It helps you build secure plans, remarkably, it's not as difficult as you may currently be believing. Someone is willing to help, this person can offer their wisdom and life experience. This gives you a helping hand towards a chapter which allows you to grow your ambitions. Your working life is moving forward towards a new assignment. News arrives, which shines a light on a new area. It helps align you towards a powerful path of potential. This leads to you moving forward, it draws a crucial moment, which gives you something to celebrate. Seeing your situation, visibly improving is a boost to your morale, it continues to deliver happy surprises which may even bring an exciting breakthrough. Your creativity is heightened to support innovative growth.

LOVE & ROMANCE

Singles Sagittarians reveal that there is a unique aspect arriving in your life soon, it does bring opportunities to socialize and does shift your focus towards sharing with another person. Open talks create a fascinating dialogue, paying attention to your intuition, you get a better idea of the potential possible with this person. Remarkably, communication is flowing freely, paving the way for a closer bond. The time is coming when you see the development of relationships occurring. Later this year is a time of heightened potential in your romantic life. It sees you embracing a significant aspect where your horizons draw you towards an area where you can connect with this individual. It is a new direction, it links you towards a happy a chapter, spending time in lively discussions with this person lights an exciting path forward. Being flexible, broadening your perception to the potential which is seeking to tempt you forward, does give you an alternative route. You are headed towards a crossroads, decisive action is going to lead to a breakthrough which delivers results, it creates space for the right environment to flourish in your personal life. This is a journey which does sweep away outworn areas and sees you embracing new options. This is someone who brings positive changes into your life, there is a focus on socializing, creating the space needed to focus on developing a bond. It is a time of moving forward, a curious sign arrives, which reveals a clue of the potential possible with this person. You find this is someone supportive, they bring a welcome change into your world, they are the sunshine after rain. You are entering a fresh cycle of potential, it does elevate your situation, a trustworthy person arrives to tempt you forward, this leads to a golden moment with one who captures your interest. You do collaborate closely with this person, and they deliver on their promises, it brings you both towards sharing experiences and planning goals together. It's a gorgeous time which has a strong influence on future events.

Couples reveal the door to communication is opening after Mercury Retrograde ends this month, you are in a time of flux and change. There is a sense of closure surrounding your life, which is drawing you towards healing. It can bring up a sentimental aspect, this helps resolve emotions and sensitivities that may have been clinging to your energy recently. Releasing outworn energy creates space for new options to flow into your world. It does lead to an expansive journey which tempts you forward. Your realistic and pragmatic approach does set the scene to create tangible results. It is a time which sees your heart guiding you towards a chapter of discovery. Moving forward towards a new level, you reach a crucial turning point, your life is reshaped, you discover a situation which promises to revolutionize your location. It is a journey which provides sustenance, abundance, and joy. You gain clarity soon and have the opportunity to fire up personal gold. This leads to a time of promise, you discover abundance and magic surrounds your creative spirit. Life becomes a whirlwind of activity, exploring this new area does take you towards a happy chapter. It does bring a fantastic bonus to your life, you spend time with your crew, and discover your relationship bond which deepens with open communication, leading the way.

IDEAS & CREATIVITY

Sagittarius is blessed with creative gold this March. Harnessing the power of the second supermoon, you are ready to be more confident and bold about achieving your dreams. With Mercury Retrograde ending on the same day, it is a strategic time of creating those plans you can develop in real-world time. Classified information is revealed, which allows you to optimize any area of your life, it does precise confusing details, and this puts you in a prominent position to advance your situation. It is good news, a project dear to your heart is given the green light to move ahead. This lights a fire of inspiration in your belly, it moves you forward towards achieving a long-awaited goal. Having a plan in place gives you stellar results. Life lights up substantially when curious information is revealed. It encourages you to shift your focus forwards, it relates to exploring the new vocation, you develop an area which makes your heart sing. It is a spectacular time which sparkles with good fortune and advancement. A secret benefactor is doing behind the scenes negotiations which benefit your cause. This leads to a trailblazing time of growth. You are someone who is dignified and can stand tall as you have achieved a lot in life. There is a new influence coming, which may impact your experience and draw you to a new area. This could see you focus on learning a curriculum which advances your situation. Pursuing your dreams does expand your horizons and may lead to a new vocation in life. This is an extraordinary time which offers you a chance to embrace an original path. A welcome surprise arrives to light the way forward. It does bring you a heightened level of potential, which sees you circulating with your group of friends. It serves up an exciting time of new ideas and creative solutions. Spending time with a like-minded crew draws happiness and abundance.

ISSUES & HURDLE

Healing is a substantial aspect of the first part of March. Mercury retrograde ends on Monday 9th, and communication issues should improve soon after. It does also see the second super moon arriving on the same day. This full Moon in Virgo helps you tap into your emotional awareness. It brings you to a time of clearing away the blockages and letting go of outworn energy. There are a few hurdles to overcome first. Life has taken a shift backward during the Mercury Retrograde phase, and there is blocked energy which is preventing forward progress. It is a time of re-evaluating your situation and letting the problematic energy to be released.

This creates space to draw a more productive and abundant chapter to come to light. It is likely to see a new section of potential unfold. While the retrograde was a downturn and did throw a spanner in the works, making it difficult to see clearly the path ahead. Now, it is a time of repose, waiting for new information to be revealed. As you work through your situation, you discover a bridge which draws better information to light. This is still in the chapter ahead, but it does suggest that things can improve, enabling progress to follow.

APRIL HOROSCOPE

ASTROLOGICAL THEME & ZODIAC ENERGY

PATIENT ~ SKILLFUL ~ MAGICAL

WORK & CAREER

You have been in a time of transformation, the Full Moon in Libra on 8th of April is a supermoon, it's also known as Hunters Moon, this delivers personal growth. Scheduling in time to follow your passions will help guide you to the correct course to further evolve your spirit. It can feel invasive when the universe is pushing your boundaries back, it's all relating to achieving a new level of potential. It takes out outworn areas and transforms your life towards abundance. Things are set to shift forward for you, there is a global aspect at play, a multinational situation benefits your life, it governs a career path which sees advancement flowing into your life through the form of stability and options to grow your home base. Success is a prominent aspect, putting your mark on new territory, you can stake your claim in an area which offers room to grow your talents. It covers all the bases, leaving you feeling proud. You are someone who thrives on new challenges, being busy and active is a happy zone, and you are set to benefit from an industrious chapter soon which offers you room to grow your environment. After all the calculating and planning, you are now being guided towards a lovely new area which sees you in your element. It does bring an active phase of growth and advancement opening in your working life, it is a productive and happy time.

LOVE & ROMANCE

If things have felt restless on the romance front, the single and looking Sagittarian can expect a new flow of energy to sweep when the supermoon in Libra occurs on the 8th of April. This incredible full moon helps shift things forward. It does lead to an expressive chapter that could bring a romantic escapade. You have been through a time of uncertainty, this has left you wondering which direction to head towards. The good news is, illumination is coming, which gives you a sure sign that you are on the correct path towards achieving a long-held dream. Happy news delivers a track which provides clarity, it translates into a progressive chapter where you can grow your options, and obtain a pleasing result. Prospects are coming into your love life, it gives you a relationship which blossoms through focused attention, spending time with this person draws heightened potential into your personal life. You enjoy an alliance which is based on mutual respect, it gives you an excellent chance to heal the past and navigate forwards towards a situation, which is serious and offers long term potential.

The Sagittarius in a relationship is entering a time which sees you adjusting to change. This can feel uncomfortable at first, as you expand your life and push back boundaries. You can expect a myriad of opportunities to come out of this chapter, it does enable you to take advantage of advancing your situation into a new area of growth. It inspires and motivates you to dream big about the possibilities. A case is revealed, this leads to a discovery where you can move forward. It puts you in direct alignment with advancing emotional goals and drawing abundance into your world through the deepening of a bond. As you get involved with an area that is profound and directly impacts your well-being, you feel you are gaining traction on your personal goals. Examining your options, thinking about the destination lets you plot a course which takes your vision further. There is expansion coming into your environment, it does light up a path which draws stability, and puts the spotlight on achieving a long thought of the dream. Making headway on your goals brings you a mighty achievement, you can feel proud about.

IDEAS & CREATIVITY

This month relates to taking stock of your situation, looking at the achievements you have obtained, this is a time of reflection, contemplation, and planning for future growth. Doing this work brings you the gift of stability, and it provides you with an insight into your long term vision. There is a heavy emphasis on creativity ahead which lets you dial in your potential, refining your art with laser precision. This month is one of inspiration, creativity, and manifestation. It is especially relevant as you are going through a significant change which shifts your focus forwards. You can understand the path ahead by using your intuition and creativity. You forge an innovative way, in alignment with your spirit, and one which drives your vision forward towards better things.

ISSUES & HURDLES

The Supermoon in Libra this month provides you with a prime time to release the past, letting go of resentments and frustrations resolves areas which have been holding you back. Employ skills of insight and intuition to unveil this secretive energy. A hidden truth from your creative unconscious allows you to see what is hidden below the surface, as you gain insight into the subtle signs that help broaden your perception. It is a month that represents solving a complex series of mysteries which will reveal to you previously hidden insights. This will result in the broader knowledge that will allow for a flow of idea to inspire your curious and questioning mind. Let go of old energy which is limiting your progress. This old outworn energy is affecting you on multiple levels, and you are urged to have faith and find a quiet place within your heart, as you surrender to the process of letting go. By releasing your expectations, you are rewarded with renewed and balanced energy. This leaves your mind free of worry, doubt, and anxiety. This is not a process that should be rushed and accept that healing does take time. It has taken many hurdles to diminish your energy to this degree, cleansing and purifying your energy during the Supermoon aids in creating space for the new potential to arrive soon afterward.

MAY HOROSCOPE

ASTROLOGICAL THEME & ZODIAC ENERGY

SPIRITED ~ TRIUMPHANT ~ PRODUCTIVE

WORK & CAREER

Mapping out new possibilities to explore, underscores your willingness to expand your life, and be open to a unique path which tempts you towards personal growth. You may decide to switch to a new area soon, this draws an opportunity to learn and grow your talents. The wheels are in motion, this brings essential changes which offer you many blessings in the chapter ahead. This is a time which sees you becoming more expressive about what you need in your life. Shedding the layers which hold you back, reveals a more positive aspect. Life blossoms under your willingness to dive in and embrace new experiences. It does chart a course towards ambitious change, luck and good fortune are your companions on this journey forward. A transition is occurring, which is the result of your willingness to be open to new experiences. You may discover the pace and rhythm of your life pick up soon, this brings a heightened potential, it sends a clear message that things are on the move for you. It results in a shift which brings a new element into your world, this elevates your options. Focusing your energy on expansion draws a unique dynamic you can appreciate. It is an essential chapter of expanding opportunities which see you diving into uncharted territory soon. New horizons beckon, they tempt you towards achieving a more robust phase of growth. It is a time of naturally evolving potential, this guides you towards a path that you can enjoy. This news is coming within weeks, it helps you reshape your goals, you can review progress, and plan a course towards a new level of growth. It is a time of focusing on an ambitious enterprise, long term plans come into view. Ultimately, you gain robust growth.

LOVE & ROMANCE

Singles can get ready for an exciting chapter which offers you room to expand your horizons. It does see the forecast offering hidden gems of potential, an event you attend brims with happy surprises. A celebration is ahead, and this is plenty of activity to keep you busy. You enjoy the pace and thrive when a new area comes calling. A gateway of energy is bringing new opportunities which make life brighter and more enjoyable. You can enjoy a more social time, and this put you in touch with kindred spirits, it draws well-being and abundance into your life. It is time you can enjoy as it has you establishing new acquaintances, and sees your social circle expanding with like-minded friends. There is some mixing of unusual energy, social gatherings crop up, which are fun and lively. It is an eventful time which coaxes you out of your usual routine, it blends beautifully with your goals, and shines a light on a radiant chapter which brings new options into your life. It is a time which resonates a theme of friendship, community, and consistency. Self-development and personal growth are heightened in this harbor of activity. New information crosses your path soon, a secret is revealed, this is a headline aspect, it has you gaining profound insight into a situation which had been confusing. It's an extraordinary time where an opportunity lands nearby, it encourages you to expand your horizons, and move out of your comfort zone. It is a time which supports learning new interests and spending time with someone compatible with your personality.

Couples this month find that there are opportunities to develop their romance. You have a natural knack for revealing the best in your partner, a moment with this person lets you shine soon when your advice is called upon, and it does shine a light on a budding situation which represents building emotional foundations and home-based stability. This turns into a bit of a soul project, helping your love interest is drawing abundance into your world. It could reveal a path of deepening this bond is approaching for you soon. This person is someone who sees your optimism soar as they brighten your life and encourage you to take a risk and expand the situation. You can set your sights on the bigger picture possible, the vision does get more evident over time, your soul-searching sees the case blossom as you gain clarity into the potential possible. It does know a situation take shape, and if you have felt adrift recently, you soon find an anchor is possible in this person as they are very grounded. Developing life goals with this one sees you regain your sense of optimism, limitless possibilities, launch you towards an expressive phase, which is magical and inspiring. It brings you to a time which is committed and puts the emphasis on developing a close tie. Summoning the courage to expand horizons with this person does provide you with the dynamic energy which nurtures the bond and enables it to grow. Together, you take things to new heights. It is a situation which occupies your thoughts and brightens your mood. This leads to an opportunity late this month which captures your heart and your spirit.

IDEAS & CREATIVITY

Its time to review the past, taking inventory helps you decide future goals. Moving in alignment with your vision does see you investing your time correctly. It enables you to discard areas which do not resonate with your higher purpose. There are adventures close by, this draws a bustling phase of activity into being, it offers enterprising options which speak to your innovative mind. This creates a shift which draws your focus forward and directs your energy towards a path which gives you joy. An enchanting chapter brings magic into your life soon. Something special is arriving for you soon. This is a heartwarming chapter which stirs new potential into your life, it gives you a reason to expand your vision and get excited about future goals. A whirlwind of enterprising energy packs your life with new options, it plants the seeds for an exciting journey to unfold. Mingling with kindred spirits have you appreciating the support and rambunctious activity in your social life. You may feel a sense of expansion, freedom, and optimism flowing into your world soon. It does see you becoming more open to new experiences, it also brings the opportunity to broaden your vision. A series of moments culminate in a heartwarming path towards achieving your vision. A slow and steady transformation is taking your aspirations to a higher level. The better you understand the inner workings of your personality, the more comfortable you create change. You are capable of incredible things, having faith in your ability to advance your life, does provide you with an ideal platform from which to project your dreams. There has been a great deal of personal growth and self-development in your life. This theme is evolving your world.

ISSUES & HURDLES

You may be unsure of which direction to focus your energy on, this is creating shifting sands of foundations, it can have you feeling uncertain and unsettled. It all begins to revolutionize your life soon, discovering an area which holds water, does shift your focus towards building solid foundations. New potential sweeps in, it moves you forward towards a stable chapter of growth. Signs ahead tug on your heartstrings, it does have you feeling sentimental and in sync with the past. You may discover serendipity makes a powerful entrance in your life soon. The magic ahead is enchanting, it draws emotional wellness, this ramps up your awareness of the spiritual world. Tuning in brings signs from above which hold true meaning. It does transform your life and nurtures your spirit. Expect a blessing soon. It opens a buffet of new options and pathways soon. This sparks an idea which has you wanting to expand your life, you get genuinely interested in an area which offers you room to grow and learn. A journey of self-discovery and wisdom is calling your name, signs are guiding this process, leading to change. It does connect you to your spiritual gifts as well as your ancestral heritage.

JUNE HOROSCOPE

ASTROLOGICAL THEME & ZODIAC ENERGY

EFFECTIVE ~ EFFICIENT ~ OBSERVANT

WORK & CAREER

Changes are coming, which give you a bevy of opportunities to explore. Surprise news arrives, which is a revelation, you let the cat out of the bag and spill the beans on an enticing tidbit of information. It can feel complicated. First, this secret reveals new information, taking time to contemplate and gain insight into what is shown does provide you with the best foot forward. You discover a blessing in disguise takes you towards a new chapter of potential. You test the waters in a new area soon, it does see improvement arriving which offers you a chance to shine. Your circumstances are shifting towards a new area, it does help you discover a path which gives room to grow your situation. Things are in motion for you, being part of this record phase of growth does offer you a valuable journey of discovery. You are determined to not give up on your dreams, even if they are challenging, also if they challenge you, keep going, take a moment daily to renew the commitment you have made to obtaining growth and success. Your willingness to negotiate past hurdles, to embrace new options and remain committed, yet flexible, will enable you to shine brightly at your chosen endeavor.

LOVE & ROMANCE

This is likely to be an intense chapter for the single Sagittarian, You are ready to move on, to go in a new direction. You are in a time of repose, it is healing necessary aspects, this is a valuable time where you create space to nurture your spirit and honor the past. A life-changing moment is ahead, this makes everything move forward, it does capture your imagination, a romantic interlude draws harmony, it's a healing influence which gives you an extra surge of motivation to follow your heart, and experiences romantic love again. Soon enough, you find your landscape harmonizes beautifully with your long-term goals. A spirit of optimism radiates outwardly from this chapter. It is the perfect time to be around kindred spirits. Spending time with your closest ties, does heightened creativity, discussing your ideas and thoughts, gives you a chance to understand the direction you are drawn towards. There are generous perks ahead which are gained by spending time with others.

For the Sagittarian in a relationship, there is a deep sense of connection with this person. This is someone with whom you feel at home in the more full world when you are with them. This person draws harmony into your world, it sees you running through a lush field which brings romance and adventure into your life. It is a freedom driven chapter, and this beams new potential into your life. It does have you focused on a successful outcome. You are headed toward a significant turning point which positions you towards a happy chapter. It does bring family gatherings, a celebration, and other social energy into play. If you have been struggling with your personal life, this is set to change, forward motion helps you connect better with the person who makes your heart sing. It gets you back in sync with developing your dreams. You are someone significant in this person's life. Your romantic partner enjoys your caring nature, they do consider meeting you as one of their luckiest days. This person feels that you draw revitalizing energy into their life, joining forces with you blends potential together, creating a sum which is a higher total when combined. This person does feel his heart is opening towards a deeper bond with you, this is something to look forward to.

IDEAS & CREATIVITY

This is a time which is ripe with new projects and dreams to inspire your mind. It does kick off a prosperous phase where you plot a course towards future goals. It is a great time to manifest a long-held dream, and having a smart strategy in place, lets you avoid common pitfalls which could derail progress. A window is opening, harmony is ready to breeze into your life. This is a great time to advance your life by expanding your horizons. Putting your ideas and intentions into action does enable robust growth which shifts your potential forward. It is a time which draws new endeavors into your life, this is especially relevant, as it harnesses your abilities and gives you a pleasant outlook for your creative talents. It is a time which improves your confidence, it gives you an option where you can speak your mind, and follow a path which feels authentic, and in alignment with where you hope to go. Following your intuition and your heart does light an unusual way, brilliant ideas, and a yearning to expand your horizons draw a happy chapter. It makes your dreams a priority. There are opportunities to connect with intuition and creativity ahead, this will help you tune into the signs from above which do run through your life.

ISSUES & HURDLES

You are given gentle grace from spirit to support you on a journey of healing. If there is an area which has tested your patience, and left you feeling frazzled, slowing down, nurturing your spirit, creates space to embrace newfound opportunities which nurture your life. There are power and strength in your soul, your vision is currently evolving. You would do well to follow your heart and trust your intuition a whole lot more than you now do. You have inherited natural gifts of awareness which are presently undervalued. Creating space to harness the emotional energy within does provide you with the insight you can trust. It brings a breath of fresh air, and new opportunities soon follow. Bridging the gap with a new approach, you interact with those you miss. These people are a source of complicated memories, it does set a tone which underscores healing is available. As you drop your guard, you reveal that it is a good thing and shall be well received. Have faith and courage that you can negotiate the path ahead with strength and grace.

JULY HOROSCOPE

ASTROLOGICAL THEME & ZODIAC ENERGY

ADVENTUROUS ~ SPIRITED ~ COURAGEOUS

WORK & CAREER

Mercury retrograde ends on July 12th, this enables blocked imaging to resolve, it opens a new flow of creativity and draws more stable growth into your workplace throughout the rest of July. Life is chaotic, a whirlwind of activity is creating a maelstrom of new options in your world soon. You can go for gold, and obtain a stellar result. This sees floodgates opening, it does put your talents on display. You score the more generous offer, and this sends out a positive signal that you are ready for advancement. This is a time where you overcome challenges and deal with the weighty responsibilities which have eaten into your free time. It is a productive chapter, it allows you to plan for the future, you may have a big decision coming up, this offers you progress. Soon after, as momentum picks up pace in the chapter ahead, you feel less hampered, and more able to follow your innovative leanings. It is a time of expansion, lingering doubts about which direction to head toward dissolve, a clear path is reached through gaining a new perspective and spending time looking at what the end result is that you are hoping to achieve. Having a target begins the process of attaining a substantial goal. You are headed towards a glorious chapter which brings options into your life, and it sets the stage for an exciting and lively phase. New information arrives in the last week which helps clear the air, it gives you insight into an area which has been problematic, and you get a big push of encouragement to keep stoking the irons of potential. It does prevent you from second-guessing and gives you a more stable foundation from which to grow your situation. Nurturing your spirit is a priority which draws abundance, it releases destabilizing doubt, and brings equilibrium into your life.

LOVE & ROMANCE

Singles see fantastic potential revealed in the areas of love and romance this July. It is a time which shows new information. It brings turning points and changes which open the gateway to a fresh start. It ignites a flame in your life when a secret is revealed, this lets you open to a new friendship, it is a bountiful time which sees a situation which has been on the back burner picking up speed. There is a great deal of communication ahead, and this draws abundance into your world. It does mark a bold beginning of an intimate bond being ignited with this individual. A series of heartfelt moments lets everything fall into place, it initiates a wave of change around your personal life. What begins as friendship takes a dramatically different turn when this person opens up to you. It does see an expansive time of soul-stirring conversations taking place which deepens a bond. Communication which had mysteriously ran ashore and faltered does begin flowing again. This potentially opens your life to a new situation. It does create a minefield of potential outcomes to navigate, resolving issues from the past, and reconnecting with someone dear to your heart, lets you enjoy a sentimental trip down memory lane. There may be some forgiveness needed to open the floodgates to new potential with this person.

Information is revealed for the Sagittarian in a relationship, this occurs at or soon after the Lunar Eclipse on July 5th, it gives you clarity about the situation with your love interest. It is a time which reveals new secrets, something which has been bottled up for too long, is shared with you. It is a surprise, it does reconnect you to a past situation, you may find it ramps up the potential with your love interest. This is a time which spotlights new information reaching you to sweep in change, it brings a transition which touches you down towards life completing a full circle. Further information comes to light, which takes you towards healing and releasing a past situation. It does see you close the door firmly on a problematic chapter, you gain insight into what has been a confusing area, it enables you to let this path go and journey towards a new area. Finding your feet again once more, you set your sights on a clear and compelling journey towards achieving your dreams. If you have felt strain in your life, you can now embrace a phase which renews your spirit, it does bring more support, enabling you to feel secure and comfortable about expanding your horizons. You finally hit your mark soon enough, and discover new options which inspire your mind. It does see a situation drawing abundance, giving you a visionary idea to develop.

IDEAS & CREATIVITY

A lunar eclipse combines with the full moon in Capricorn. This is the Wolf Moon and is an important event which draws creative inspiration to light.

This is an ideal time to reevaluate your goals and prioritize developing a situation which holds meaning to you. It does see a productive chapter ahead, this takes you into your zone and enables you to complete a phase of incredible advancement. This sparks new options, things come together nicely, with a creative flourish. Your focus is shifting towards a journey of growth and discovery. Focusing on your goals enables you to ascertain a path which is paved with new options. It is a glittering time of discovering opportunities which offer room to grow your life. Taking advantage of these options sees you dazzle with inspiration and enthusiasm, as you connect with your personal vision. You enter phase which sees restrictions are lifted, it leads to a time of freedom, liberation, and adventure. As you make incredible tracks on improving your life, you achieve a stream of creativity which brightens your life with refreshing options. This is a fantastic time to shift your focus forwards. Growth is likely, an opportunity on the horizon brings a more grounded phase, which represents stability.

ISSUES & HURDLES

Saturn makes an entrance on July 20th, this coincides with the new Moon in Cancer. Stepping away from the hectic aspect of your life does let you process some difficult energy which has limited your potential recently. Spending time nurturing your spirit leads to rejuvenation, it does place you in the box seat to obtain a sunnier aspect. A yearning to expand your life draws new options soon, your subconscious is working overtime to guide you forwards. You are in a time of transformation, this is not easy, it is creating a critical phase where you do inner work, you can head towards a page-turning direction in your life, and as you strengthen the foundations in your world, you have an opportunity to heal parts of your life which have felt at odds recently. Things have been difficult, but you need to let that stuff go and just make life happen for a while. Trust the universe to support you during this time of repose. It does shift your focus towards healing and lets you dream about future goals to put into place in the chapter ahead. This is an excellent time to take inventory, really examine your current situation, look at where you've come from, and think about where you are headed. It does let you resolve outworn areas, and it removes the stuck energy that you simply don't need in your life anymore. Creating space to prioritize your goals, sees a shift forward, it benefits your life, and advances your situation. Nurturing your dreams is your ticket to happiness, dream big and go for it.

AUGUST HOROSCOPE

Astrological Theme & Zodiac Energy

Inventive ~ Knowledgeable ~ Provocative

Work & Career

It's time for a change, this activates a highly creative and growth orientated phase. It does bring new demands and a role with added responsibilities, your changing situation offers a chance to grow your talents. It does require initiative as thinking on your feet lets you make the most of this enterprising journey. A cohesive plan soon takes shape, it about building strong foundations, as you gain a foothold up to a new level of potential. This is a time which motivates a fresh start, it does see epic potential arriving to grow your gifts in a new area. Making a commitment to stoke the fires of your inspiration gives you a leg up to a new pathway. An offer arrives, which sparks an active phase of growth, you pick up speed, and soon deal with a hectic environment, you thrive in this vital area, the conditions are right to achieve a stellar outcome. You kickstart a new area soon, this puts a spotlight on growing your career path, it brings essential collaborations, new options lead to an active phase of growth. It does see you qualify for an ambitious change, you reveal new potential, and team up with other dynamic and enterprising people who understand the inner workings of ambition. It brings together creativity and innovation to stunning effect.

Love & Romance

Singles enter a social aspect which has you spending time with a kindred spirit, and this develops a bond, the interactions with this person are fresh and lively, you feel in sync with this individual, this is someone who seems like a soulmate. Expanding your horizons and taking a chance in love brings you to an expansive time, you explore a budding new situation, which has you more expressive and confident than you have been for some time. It connects you with a path which draws abundance. An enlightening conversation takes place, you unearth a new dynamic, this is especially relevant for your love life. It does let you go to a chapter of adventure and expansion. It illuminates close communication with one who offers you game-changing potential. Chemistry, which has been brewing over recent months spills over into a more bonded and committed situation. It does have you exploring new territory with one who can deliver results. More is yet to come in your personal life. Don't sweat on the timeline, put your energy towards the future with a clear and convincing intention. Potential soars through your life through your willingness to open your heart. It results in things coming together nicely when the time is right for you both. You can set your sights on a future which is abundant and leads to the renewal of bonds. Priorities and plans come into focus.

The Sagittarian with a relationship sees that impressive results are likely to blaze through your personal life soon. This leads to an attraction which heats up the potential possible in your life. There is a heartwarming moment, which is expressive and open, it does bring emotions up to be shared. All in all, your life is flowing towards harmony, drawing abundance, and shower your life with blessings. Your patience is rewarded with a shift forward, this brings things together, it draws inspiration, and incorporates strategies which enable growth to occur. Raising the bar of excellence does set the stage for impressive results. It takes you to new depths of emotions and bonding, it awakens you to a new level of potential. There is an undercurrent of chemistry ready to blossom in your personal life. A game-changing conversation ahead sees a situation level up, it soars to the next level of commitment. This is a time which liberates fear and doubt, it feels magical, not confining or restrictive. It does draw a bond which creates a new dynamic, this sees a shift of perspective, you deepen a relationship with someone willing to contribute fully and open the heart to a deeper situation. This sets the stage for nurturing closer ties.

IDEAS & CREATIVITY

You switch into manifestation mode when news arrives, which tempts you to shift your focus forward. You are ready to create change, it blends perfectly with a spontaneous chapter that activates creativity, and draws new options to bring abundance into your world. Your perseverance, persistence, and discipline are rewarded, it does bring a project which provides you with a beautiful outlet to focus your excess energy into. This is a time of nurturing and growing your life, taking time to develop an area of interest does get a situation of the ground, take full advantage of that which seeks to shift your focus forwards. It is a move in the right direction, and this enables you to grow something special, it is a time of new ideas and information, it provides you with much-needed clarity about an area which inspires and motivates. It's all coming about due to your willingness to enter uncharted territory. This expansion has been percolating in the background of your life for some time, now you discover, a gateway opens to take you towards the achievement of a dream. It does see you release self-sabotaging patterns which only limit your potential. You heed the call of the wild and create a significant shift in your lifestyle, which has you feeling excited. This track governs self-expression, creativity, and personal freedom. It's an area which speaks of being authentic, not just to others, but to yourself. Creating outlets which let you capture the essence of your personality does grow that which seeks expression in your everyday world. You have a keen eye for opportunities, don't be held back, keep expanding and nurturing your talents, an offer may arise soon to ignite inspiration in a new area.

ISSUES & HURDLES

This is a time which brings a great chance to integrate various elements of your life, you absorb and resolve emotions which have complicated your life. Soul-searching brings a few epiphanies about areas which need work, and also where to shift your focus next. Releasing the past opens the door on a lighter and brighter future. It's has you emerging from a difficult chapter, ready to embrace a new flow of potential. Something may not be entirely transparent, but to sit tight, you will discover insight into the situation shortly. If you have weathered a few storms this year, you can close the door on a chapter which feels done with, it does bring you to a new path which offers room to grow your life. Processing and releasing the past creates space for a more abundant flow of energy to arrive soon enough. This is a time which stirs up a nostalgic view, it can trigger sensitive feelings, this is an emotional time, untangling your thoughts and feelings is an integral part of gaining insight and clarity into the path ahead. If you are feeling confused or unsettled, it is a sign that there is unresolved energy to work on. This prompts you to revisit your situation and reevaluate specific goals and areas. You are kind and gracious, someone who gives freely of their time. Your soft heart and sense of compassion draw others into your world. Paying attention to nurturing your spirit does help alleviate any reason for burnout, which may burden your energy when you give more than you receive. It's also important to reach out to your support network and get a little help from friends.

SEPTEMBER HOROSCOPE

Astrological Theme & Zodiac Energy

Versatile ~ Durable ~ Skillful

Work & Career

You open new leads. It positioned you perfectly to explore a home-based business. It enables you to fortify and stabilize your home situation. A breath of fresh air draws abundance into your world. This is a shift which creates positive change and opens a gateway towards a happier environment. You can cut corners to obtain your goals, plus there's a less overall expense when you focus on home life as well. This is a time which draws new information. It does offer you impressive results and takes your dreams up a notch. It is an influence which flows through your life to inspire growth and change. This is a beautiful theme which positions you correctly to learn an area of interest, it does expand what is possible in your life. It does advance your situation, as an influx of opportunities is flowing into your life soon. This is a time where you elevate your profile in your chosen industry. It does offer a more prosperous working environment, and this adds security and growth to your chart. It may bring a breakthrough which rewards you with a new role. Being open to the path ahead draws advancement into your working life. It does trigger an active phase of potential over the coming month. It's a time for big sky dreaming, a sunny aspect is going to fling open the door to potential soon. As you lift the shutters on areas which have limited progress, you see positive signs that much is possible in the chapter ahead. It does directly align you towards advancement, this is a time of steady development where you can accomplish a robust result. It has you feeling proud and inspired.

Love & Romance

Those who are single and looking for love, discover that their social life is going to be a source of vibrant and dynamic elements in the chapter ahead. If you felt things have been an uphill battle recently, you can enjoy more freedom in your life soon. It does liberate restrictions and leads to an expansive and expressive phase of developing social bonds. A situation in your social circle blossoms and you get involved with an ambitious project which has you working closely with another. You enter a social time which draws lively invitations, and activities. It does see events cropping up which have you mingling with others in your social circle. There is plenty of communication and lively discussions ahead, it is an expansive time which draws positive options into your world. With plenty of invitations to choose from, you feel in control of the path ahead. It is an expressive and enjoyable chapter.

An opportunity appears in your life soon, this positions you brilliantly towards a new chapter. Your efforts to improve your circumstances, bear fruit, a harvest arrives, which gives you tangible feedback. It does lead to a celebration, you can relax and renew your spirit with friends and family. It does bring a path which glimmers with new options to explore. It's something which strengthens family ties, it helps release the intense feelings you've had in your life recently, things begin to lighten up, it clears space for a more joyful and abundant chapter. It sees better foundations in your home life, this brings a stronger connection with your closest ties, it does see conversations occurring which facilitate growth, working through situations with constructive dialogue creates positive change. There is new potential arriving in sweeping fresh energy. You may have found things have been stale recently, this is set to change, you discover a bond is possible with emotionally receptive one, this person reconnects you with an exact situation. It is a time for bonding. Being authentic and transparent sees a stronger, more durable bond being forged. It is cast with titanium, able to last the distance, this creates a sacred environment where you can merge towards a more profound and intimate climate. It's bringing desires together and sharing heartfelt conversations, expressions of love bring magic and awakening to your personal life. Fireworks and chemistry ignite, creating spectacular romantic potential.

IDEAS & CREATIVITY

This is a rare and curious time which sees new information revealed, as you move towards a new zone, you prepare to transition forward while keeping a sense of balance. The winds of change blow in, they carry you towards new opportunities, it does see a breakthrough moment arriving, which may put you in a tailspin of excitement. Anticipating a step ahead helps you navigate deftly through this fantastic time. It is a lucrative time to expand your horizons, take a risk in a new venture, and it could lead to a business opportunity which helps you craft your talents to a new level. Getting your abilities out to a broader audience broadens the scope of potential possible. It does take your vision to a new level, this is an exciting time which offers fascinating and curious pathways towards growth. Something new and tempting arrives to inspire your mind. It brings you to an area, which is refreshing and abundant, this is a time that can heal outworn energy, it transforms your life by shifting your focus forwards, and taking you to a happier chapter. This gifts your life with new options, you discover the right path to skip down. It widens your vision as new possibilities take shape. You make some discoveries which broaden your horizons and take you to a broader world of opportunity. It does see a shift forward which integrates new options into your life. This makes you go out of your comfort zone, it does transform your life, which leads to a happier chapter. It is a phase of reinvention, creating change inspires your mind, and this gives you an open path to explore, new adventures soon call your name.

ISSUES & HURDLES

You possess high strength, it is from within you get your fortitude and resilience. This enables you to take an innovative approach and overcome hurdles, you capitalize on the power of your heritage, and can achieve a stellar outcome with your willingness to persevere. Putting in serious work draws a higher magnitude of opportunities into your life soon. This is a time where you can review your progress, there may be issues which have unnecessarily impeded your progress recently, discovering pathways to streamline does lead to a more productive and progressive chapter. It is a valuable time to navigate correctly towards your goals, using strategy does plot a course which sees a successful result been obtained. A decision is made soon, which starts a dynamic new cycle. As you press forward towards your goals, you create significant change, the power of strength blossoms in your spirit to assist you in reaching for a substantial purpose. It does help you break free of limiting constraints and release the anxiety and doubt. The winds of change propel you forward. Clear skies enter into your life soon, this opens the pathway ahead, it does connect you to your real creativity which seeks to reveal itself in your world. Manifesting tangible results does provide you with a beautiful outlet you can appreciate. If you have been dealing with severe life changes, doing some work which nurtures your spirit will draw dividends.

OCTOBER HOROSCOPE

ASTROLOGICAL THEME & ZODIAC ENERGY

AWARE ~ IDEALISTIC ~ ADAPTIVE

WORK & CAREER

You are going through a time of transition and change, this can feel unsettling, setting your sights on those long term plans, help you focus your energy correctly, achieving your goals becomes a top priority, this sees potential soaring through your life, it helps you get your grand vision off the ground. Flexing new strategies provide you with innovative solutions, nailing your master plan leads to success. You enter a time which sees growth is possible, it does highlight a new role, being willing to advocate and advance your situation, does invite an offer which inspires and delights. Things work in your favor, change is arriving, which secures a better result. You reveal a new responsibility is possible. It does bring you to a new level of potential within your career. An opportunity crops up to create a substantial shift forward. It hits the ticket to a trailblazing chapter where you make significant progress on your larger goals. This is a time of transitions, the winds of change blow in, and they carry you towards new foundations. As you move forward, you stabilize and organize your life in new surroundings. It is a practical and productive chapter, with many projects ahead.

LOVE & ROMANCE

Your intuition plays an important role this month for singles, and as you can envision things coming together, it gives you a sense of knowing future events before they happen. You are correct, things will unfold fully when the time is right for progression. This situation will blossom when the time is right, it does see fortune shining on your personal life. You transition towards a time which draws abundance. It does bring on a chapter which is exciting and adventurous, you reveal a bond as possible with the one who is magnetic, charming, and captivating. There may be some uncertainty and confusion around this area, but breaking free of constraints soon brings you into uncharted territory. It does enable foundations to be built, which restores peace and tranquility. It is a significant life change, this person discovers a newfound sense of confidence, capability, and inspiration. It brings the situation forward, things progress, and it opens a new room of possibilities which are fantastic and offer them a place to clear the decks and embrace a forward-thinking chapter. It does see improvements arriving which bring blessings.

Sagittarians in a relationship finds that Mercury Retrograde delivers a bump in the road when it arrives on the 13th, you can navigate around it by being flexible. While Mercury Retrograde does throw a spanner in the works and creates unnecessary complications in your current situation, sharing openly with this person does set the scene for issues to be resolved. It is a bit of a minefield, a tricky path can be negotiated with honesty and direct communication. Your partner is tolerant and intrigued, this person wants to know precisely what is going on with this situation. Channel your love into the bond, and it will grow. Things begin to become cozier when new energy enters your personal life. It leads to more of a domestic situation, the love and affection you pour into this situation, brings powerful bonding which enables a beautiful case to flourish. It does lead to long-term goals taking shape, you open your heart to progressing a meaningful case with the one who inspires your heart, it leads to magical moments ahead.

IDEAS & CREATIVITY

You transition towards a significant event which is positive, but difficult in the short term. Mercury Retrogrades appearance creates a shift which requires strength, and fortitude. However, this blessing in disguise leads to a glorious outcome, you do discover a richly abundant path, heighten opportunities light a new journey forward. This sees you expanding your vision, it enables you to harness wild and rebellious energy, and enjoy a chapter of new adventures. You are given the grace to expand your horizons out of your comfort zone. There is an area which has been testing your patience, things will resolve, it does see progress being made after a time of waiting for new information to arrive. You carve out time to focus your energy on areas which draw improvement. It does bring a chapter ruled by imagination and creativity, you discover results are possible using innovative solutions. News arrives, which bring new options into your life. It does create a whirlwind of potential, this can feel chaotic, it gives you a boost, you can push forward to a new level of potential. There is an experimental flavor to this time of year, you can set in motion different paths, and go with the flow, discovering through trial and error, the right route to develop fully. It does lead to a life-changing chapter which holds fantastic potential.

ISSUES & HURDLES

There is a need for patience, balance, and perspective this month. It is essential to allow time for your creative ideas to germinate in the womb of your consciousness. Don't try to force or rush positive change in your life during the Mercury Retrograde phase, but gently guide this process forward. Understanding the essence of how this energy can block and restrict your progress, allows you to make peace with the holdup. It enables you to resolve blocks which frustrate and further delay your forward motion. Spend time creating space for a cathartic release of emotional healing, it brings a new day dawning by month's end, and the sun soon shines once again.

NOVEMBER HOROSCOPE

Astrological Theme & Zodiac Energy

Idealistic ~ Deep ~ Aware

Work & Career

Change is coming, new options provide you with exciting advancement, this correlates beautifully with a long-held goal. As you charge ahead, lingering doubts are released, you feel a sense of courage and confidence empower your spirit. It revolutionizes your vision and broadens your perception of what can be achieved. Taking proactive measures to improve your life, you score a lucrative situation. You have an incredible hunger for knowledge, it does draw new goals to light soon. A visionary idea sparks a wildfire of potential. This leads to an opportunity which comes out of the blue, but provide you with a good fit for your skills. Expanding your life brings your talents to a new level. You can embrace the challenges ahead and know that you can bring things towards a successful outcome. Something is arriving for you soon which helps you feel a greater sense of security, it resolves an issue which may have been problematic, and it does emphasize new options arriving which help you manifest a strategy to achieve a long term goal. It's all a shift forwards, this fuels an exciting chapter, it takes your talents to a new level. Work. This is an excellent time to review your options and begin to plot a course towards an ambitious goal. Full steam ahead is coming soon to shift your focus forward. It does anchor you in a productive chapter, you are grounded, and ready to start putting your goals into action. During this practical cycle, you shift into an active mode, your ideas and vision take form and bring joy.

Love & Romance

Singles reveal that things are on the move for when you run into someone you haven't seen for some time. It provides you with a light-hearted moment, and quite a bit to catch up on. There are many beneficial aspects to the chapter ahead, it does draw more social opportunities, which heightens your sense of well-being. The feeling of being connected with others is a theme which runs especially strong through your life. It brings you a wonderful sense of togetherness soon. It is a chapter which expands the boundaries of your life. You can draw in fresh inspiration, and this is cathartic to your soul. Outworn areas are no longer problematic, you are willing to look ahead and embrace the development of substantial goals. Life picks up the pace, and you can trust your instincts to reliably guide you forward. Honoring that voice within, you receive information subliminally which points to the correct area for progression.

Those in a relationship find that flexibility and compassion bring balance into the equation. The stability is secured through a greater understanding of what each other needs. There is a sense of this person needing more personal freedom to creatively express themselves. Opening your heart to expanding horizons and focusing on setting attainable goals will help keep the situation flowing forward. Security and stability are ahead for this relationship. The chapter ahead is softer and sweeter for you. It draws a sense of balance which allows you to create space to nurture your spirit. It is a social time, which sees invitations arrive to engage with your broader community. You benefit from being surrounded by kindred spirits, the atmosphere is lively and draws abundance into your world. Honoring your intuitive side provides you with added benefits to uncover a new path of growth.

IDEAS & CREATIVITY

You launch into an active phase of growth and development, tapping into new opportunities, you get a creative project off the ground. It is a time which elevates your talents, rising above the competition lets you stand out, and your work is noticed. It draws a legitimate offer which has you thinking big about the possibilities, a compelling path opens, tempting you forward. It is an unpredictable time which brings an exciting avenue to explore. Luckily, you are ready for a new adventure. Expanding your horizons is a priority, your inner compass is guiding you towards a new journey of growth. You gain insight and clarity into the path ahead, this gives your confidence boost, pushing back the barriers, creates space for exciting new options to shift your focus forward. It's not a matter of if but when this shift takes place. Making this a priority does quicken the process. Focusing on making it happen, you discover an option arrives to complement your plans. You get your bearings in a new environment, it does take time to fully manifest this potential, a big transition is coming, it sees foundations being built which offer you room to grow your life. Timing is the key to everything, perhaps work has been problematic this year, you are given a new option soon, which draws a better environment. It does see new learning taking place, you dedicate yourself to fine-tuning your abilities, and improving your circumstances. Achieving mastery in your chosen field leads to a breakthrough, it allows you to branch out into a new area.

Issues & Hurdles

The problematic energy eases as Mercury Retrograde ends on the 3rd. However, it may leave you feeling unsettled, anxious, and a sense of disquiet. You are ready to release the holding pattern which has kept you stuck. This paves the way for a substantial chapter which allows opportunities to come through that perfectly align to your spirit. The actions you take during this time have the power to be developed further over the coming months. It does place you in an enviable position, you can garner experience and a deeper understanding of what you are hoping to achieve in your world. Mysterious, and enigmatic energy is around you during the New Moon in Scorpio on the 15th, it may lead you to question a situation that is deeply woven into your unconscious. You may experience haunting thoughts and emotions during the lunar phase, as the path ahead is clouded. These emotions are part of the rich tapestry of life, and this darker side gives you a greater understanding of yourself, it allows you to let go of your blockages by incorporating them into this time. The New Moon provides you with a time of gentle grace where that which feels comfortable in the darkness can emerge to be safely acknowledged. You heal hidden aspects of yourself, by accepting and understanding their presence, allows your energy to be renewed once the moon grows into it's a full lantern on the 30th.

DECEMBER HOROSCOPE

ASTROLOGICAL THEME & ZODIAC ENERGY

IRREPRESSIBLE ~ EXCITING ~ HECTIC

WORK & CAREER

You are entering a vital time relating to your career path. It does suggest a professional opportunity is arriving soon, this gives you a fantastic reward for the work you have undertaken this year. It is an exciting time where you can enjoy elevating your prospects. A new assignment gives you a great new area to concentrate your talents on. It does begin a stable phase of growth and advancement. Things are on the move at work. It does bring something new, which gives you a chance to grow your career. Doing your best on an upcoming project leads you towards growth, it gives you recognition, and the feedback provides you with insight into where your capabilities are taking you. There is an offer coming to negotiate, it draws incredible benefits, showing your best side may score you a new role. It triggers an active phase for you, this influence does bring achievements, you reveal a lucky career break which you have worked hard for. As this makes an appearance in your life, a door opens towards advancement. This is a nice boost to your professional life, it elevates your situation, and lets others see your ability to shine in the workplace. It creates space for something new, you are ready to handle more, and will enjoy the challenge. There are changes ahead for your career path, it has you feeling excited as you become involved in learning a new area. This beautifully aligns you towards growth, it has you merging with other successful types, and this brings remarkable stability into your world. It all has a part to play in achieving personal growth and discovering new options. An opportunity arrives to shift your situation forward, it brings a gift of stability and long-term security, this is a busy time, it sees you tying up loose ends, and organizing your life to create a steadily improving environment. You will feel the benefits of this chapter over a longer time, as it continues to draw happiness into your life.

LOVE & ROMANCE

December does look promising for those who are single and looking for love, it is a positive chapter for personal growth. You crack the code on a new chapter in your own life. Invitations crop up out of the blue, this sees you mingling with some new people, introductions are made which lead to a lively time of sharing discussions. This spontaneous time brings the spark back into your world, it's easy making headway on your goals, and it provides you with scope to progress, a situation which has you thinking about the potential possible. An exciting moment with another at a social event shines a light on the area of developing a bond. This brings an exciting phase of romantic potential into your world. It does see you exploring synergies with someone perceptive. It leaves you feeling pleasant, it has the potential to flourish dramatically.

Those in a relationship may find that talking with your love interest about your concerns or views about where this relationship should be headed can be a source of tension, approaching the bond gracefully and with compassion, does resolve issues which have impeded progress. It is a situation which has a tendency to not reach full throttle, if this person has been half-hearted with their commitment, organizing, streamlining, and patience will stabilize the foundations, and create a trend which sees forward growth occurring. You find your equilibrium with this person, having shared goals, taking time to let potential unfold naturally, all places you in the box seat to improve a bond which holds meaning. You prioritize developing your life, it is a time where personal goals come into focus, and opportunities ahead to give you a reason to celebrate the success achieved. Working on your relationship draws tangible results which are heartwarming. It does see your love life is set to burn brightly during the Solar eclipses on the 14th. This offers you an influx of new potential. It does lead to a time of better merging your goals on a deeper level with this person. It opens a myriad of possibilities to explore and leads to a romantic connection which is stronger and more in sync with your shared dreams.

IDEAS & CREATIVITY

December is a month which provides you with heightened creative powers. This illuminate's all that was previously hidden in darkness, and this fire energy of creation expands your horizons and invigorates you with inspired thinking, and increased self-confidence. Feelings of brilliance, power, and higher consciousness help guide your path forward. Insight and innovative thinking help you to harness the power of your creative ideas and allow them to take shape in the physical world. As you give form to your visualizations, you combine fire energy with grounded earthiness. This represents heaven and earth coming together to inspire new dreams. As you radiate on a higher vibrational level this month, you harness the power of creativity that is within to plot a course for next years goals. This is also a month of quiet reflection and introspection. Looking within will help you gain awareness into which direction you want to focus your creative energy. It broadens your consciousness and raises your perception of what is needed in your life. There is a need to turn away from the external world if you find the holiday season too hectic and chaotic. This time of reflection will provide you with the clarity that will illuminate a path forward for you. It is in the stillness, quietness that you will hear your inner guide. After a draining a few weeks, spending time with loved ones refuels your energy, it draws renewal into your spirit. It is the season for reflection, especially during the winter solstice on the 21st. This guide you to maintain balance, and plan of thoughtfully towards your future goals. A celebration at months and has you feeling inspired and excited about life.

ISSUES & HURDLES

There is an undercurrent of transformation occurring in your life, the year is complete, it has been eventful, it has been a journey into growth and learning. Your quest is not over, it is only just beginning. You are given space during the solstice on the 21st to reflect on the difficulties you have faced, the hurdles you are overcome, and the strength you have drawn close to your chest this year. As you reveal the cracks in your life, you realize that there is more work to be done, then a simple patch-up job. It is a call to nurture your spirit, to make yourself a priority, and to deal with any part of your life that has been swept under the rug. If you have blocked energy holding your progress back, it will serve you well to create space to honor this energy and release it. It is a time where you can find your power by doing inner work. Working on your emotional terrain is going to revolutionize your potential. It underscores a theme of change, healing, and evolution, which is flowing around your situation, guiding you to take more significant steps forward, do the work, which is necessary, and reap the results. He feels that you undervalue your potential, a great deal can be achieved through expanding your horizons into virgin territory. Explore new pathways to growth.

ASTROLOGICAL DIARY

2020

Astrological Diary

2020

Time is set to Coordinated Universal Time Zone (UT±0)

January

Mon 30

Tues 31

Wed 1
New Year's Day

Thurs 2

January

Fri 3
First Quarter Moon in Aries. 4.45 UTC
Quadrantids Meteor Shower. Jan 1st-5th. Peaks night of Jan 3rd.

Sat 4

Sun 5

Notes
Lucky Numbers: 11, 62, 12, 61, 32, 5
Astrological Energy: Experiential
Color: White

January

Mon 6

Tues 7

Wed 8

Thurs 9

January

Fri 10

Full Moon in Cancer. Wolf Moon. 19:21 UTC
Penumbral Lunar Eclipse.

Sat 11

Sun 12

Notes

Lucky Numbers: 23, 30, 22, 15, 27, 11
Astrological Energy: Directed
Color: Bone

January

Mon 13

Tues 14

Wed 15

Thurs 16

January

Fri 17

Last Quarter Moon in Libra. 12.58 UTC

Sat 18

Sun 19

Notes

Lucky Numbers: 32, 88, 26, 40, 92, 85
Astrological Energy: Optimistic
Color: Sky Blue

January

Mon 20
Martin Luther King Day

Tues 21

Wed 22

Thurs 23

January

Fri 24
New Moon in Capricorn. 21:42 UTC

Sat 25
Chinese New Year (Rat)

Sun 26
Last Quarter Moon in Scorpio. 21.10 UTC

Notes
Lucky Numbers: 27, 95, 10, 77, 23, 2
Astrological Energy: Visionary
Color: Indigo

January

Mon 27

Tues 28

Weds 29

Thurs 30

January/February

Fri 31

Sat 1
Imbolc

Sun 2
First Quarter Moon in Taurus. 1.42 UTC.
Groundhog Day

Notes
Lucky Numbers: 80, 11, 88, 22, 68, 99
Astrological Energy: Influential
Color: Violet

February

Mon 3

Tues 4

Weds 5

Thurs 6

February

Fri 7

Sat 8

Sun 9
Full Moon in Leo, Supermoon. Snow Moon. 7:33 UTC

Notes
Lucky Numbers: 31, 16, 96, 44, 21, 26
Astrological Energy: Commanding
Color: Midnight Blue

February

Mon 10

Mercury at largest Eastern Elongation.

Tues 11

Weds 12

Thurs 13

February

Fri 14
Valentine's Day

Sat 15
Last Quarter Moon in Scorpio. 22.17 UTC

Sun 16

Notes
Lucky Numbers: 93, 70, 24, 17, 39, 52
Astrological Energy: Imaginative
Color: Royal Blue

February

Mon 17
Presidents' Day

Tues 18
Mercury Retrograde begins

Weds 19

Thurs 20

February

Fri 21

Sat 22

Sun 23

New Moon in Aquarius. 15:32 UTC

Notes

Lucky Numbers: 49, 52, 8, 43, 85, 76
Astrological Energy: Adventurous
Color: Gold

February

Mon 24

Tues 25
Shrove Tuesday (Mardi Gras)

Weds 26
Ash Wednesday

Thurs 27

February/March

Fri 28

Sat 29

Sun 1

Notes

Lucky Numbers: 24, 67, 64, 94, 96, 55
Astrological Energy: Vivacious
Color: Yellow

March

Mon 2

First Quarter Moon in Gemini. 19.57 UTC

Tues 3

Weds 4

Thurs 5

March

Fri 6

Sat 7

Sun 8

Notes

Lucky Numbers: 84, 50, 93, 9, 48, 8
Astrological Energy: Productive
Color: Hot Pink

March

Mon 9
Full Moon in Virgo, Supermoon. Worm Moon. 17:48 UTC
Mercury Retrograde ends.
Purim (begins at sundown)

Tues 10
Purim (ends at sundown)

Weds 11

Thurs 12

March

Fri 13

Sat 14

Sun 15

Notes

Lucky Numbers: 27, 62, 37, 49, 90, 69
Astrological Energy: Passionate
Color: Cyan

March

Mon 16

Last Quarter Moon in Sagittarius. 9.34 UTC

Tues 17

St Patrick's Day

Wed 18

Thurs 19

March

Fri 20
Ostara/Spring Equinox. 3:50 UTC

Sat 21

Sun 22

Notes
Lucky Numbers: 74, 38, 95, 88, 2, 72
Astrological Energy: Constructive
Color: Spring Green

March

Mon 23

Tues 24

Mercury at most substantial Western Elongation.
Venus at most substantial Eastern Elongation.
New Moon in Aries. 9:28 UTC

Weds 25

Thurs 26

March

Fri 27

Sat 28

Sun 29

Notes

Lucky Numbers: 3, 93, 58, 91, 27, 81
Astrological Energy: Trusting
Color: Rose

March/April

Mon 30

Tues 31

Weds 1

First Quarter Moon in Cancer. 10.21 UTC
All Fools/April Fools Day

Thurs 2

April

Fri 3

Sat 4

Sun 5
Palm Sunday

Notes
Lucky Numbers: 3, 66, 5, 74, 53, 82
Astrological Energy: Celebratory
Color: Lemon

April

Mon 6

Tues 7

Weds 8

Full Moon in Libra, Supermoon. Pink Moon. 2:35 UTC
Passover (begins at sunset)

Thurs 9

April

Fri 10
Good Friday

Sat 11

Sun 12
Easter Sunday

Notes
Lucky Numbers: 86, 33, 34, 35, 75, 61
Astrological Energy: Harmonious
Color: Amber

April

Mon 13

Tues 14
Last Quarter Moon in Capricorn. 22.56 UTC

Weds 15

Thurs 16
Passover ends

April

Fri 17
Orthodox Good Friday

Sat 18

Sun 19
Orthodox Easter

Notes
Lucky Numbers: 37, 65, 90, 62, 99, 5
Astrological Energy: Inspiring
Color: Baby Blue

April

Mon 20

Tues 21

Weds 22

Lyrids Meteor Shower. April 16th-25th. Peaks night of April 22nd.
Earth Day

Thurs 23

New Moon in Taurus. 2:26 UTC
Ramadan Begins

April

Fri 24

Sat 25

Sun 26

Notes

Lucky Numbers: 88, 39, 83, 85, 26, 28
Astrological Energy: Committed
Color: Honeydew

April

Mon 27

Tues 28

Weds 29

Thurs 30
First Quarter Moon in Leo. 20.38 UTC

May

Fri 1
Beltane/May Day

Sat 2

Sun 3

Notes
Lucky Numbers: 18, 15, 51, 13, 41, 1
Astrological Energy: Complex
Color: Deep Pink

May

Mon 4

Tues 5

Weds 6
Eta Aquarids Meteor Shower. April 19th - May 28th. Peaks night of May 6th.

Thurs 7
Full Moon in Scorpio, Supermoon. Flower Moon. 10:45 UTC

May

Fri 8

Sat 9

Sun 10
Mother's Day

Notes
Lucky Numbers: 43, 65, 59, 5, 54, 34
Astrological Energy: Productive
Color: Forest Green

May

Mon 11

Tues 12

Weds 13

Thurs 14
Last Quarter Moon in Aquarius. 14.03 UTC

May

Fri 15

Sat 16

Sun 17

Notes

Lucky Numbers: 11, 68, 9, 39, 20, 88
Astrological Energy: Vibrant
Color: Aqua

May

Mon 18

Victoria Day (Canada)

Tues 19

Weds 20

Thurs 21

May

Fri 22
New Moon in Taurus. 17:39 UTC

Sat 23
Ramadan Ends

Sun 24

Notes
Lucky Numbers: 81, 34, 21, 97, 66, 43
Astrological Energy: Courageous
Color: Dark Violet

May

Mon 25
Memorial Day

Tues 26

Weds 27

Thurs 28
Shavuot (begins at sunset)

May

Fri 29

Sat 30
First Quarter Moon in Virgo. 3.30 UTC
Shavuot (ends at sunset)

Sun 31

Notes
Lucky Numbers: 29, 85, 92, 91, 60, 30
Astrological Energy: Complex
Color: Slate Blue

June

Mon 1

Tues 2

Weds 3

Thurs 4
Mercury at Greatest Eastern Elongation.

June

Fri 5
Full Moon in Sagittarius. Strawberry Moon. 19:12 UTC
Penumbral Lunar Eclipse.

Sat 6

Sun 7

Notes
Lucky Numbers: 74, 57, 56, 75, 67, 33
Astrological Energy: Daring
Color: Straw

June

Mon 8

Tues 9

Weds 10

Jupiter at Opposition.

Thurs 11

June

Fri 12

Sat 13
Last Quarter Moon in Pisces. 6.24 UTC

Sun 14
Flag Day

Notes
Lucky Numbers: 24, 61, 96, 42, 88, 47
Astrological Energy: Active
Color: Fire Brick

June

Mon 15

Tues 16

Weds 17

Mercury Retrograde begins.

Thurs 18

June

Fri 19

Sat 20

Sun 21

New Moon in Cancer. 6:41 UTC
Midsummer/Litha Solstice. 21:44 UTC
Annual Solar Eclipse.
Father's Day

Notes

Lucky Numbers: 21, 96, 92, 61, 36, 70
Astrological Energy: Exciting
Color: Cornflower Blue

June

Mon 22

Tues 23

Weds 24

Thurs 25

June

Fri 26

Sat 27

Sun 28
First Quarter Moon in Libra. 8.16 UTC

Notes
Lucky Numbers: 5, 91, 69, 39, 64, 6
Astrological Energy: Creative
Color: Red

June/July

Mon 29

Tues 30

Weds 1
Canada Day

Thurs 2

July

Fri 3
Independence Day (observed)

Sat 4
Independence Day

Sun 5
Full Moon in Capricorn. Buck Moon 4:44 UTC
Penumbral Lunar Eclipse.

Notes
Lucky Numbers: 58, 40, 99, 95, 18, 92
Astrological Energy: Curious
Color: Orange

July

Mon 6

Tues 7

Weds 8

Thurs 9

July

Fri 10

Sat 11

Sun 12
Last Quarter Moon in Aries. 23.29 UTC
Mercury Retrograde ends.

Notes
Lucky Numbers: 7, 36, 2, 20, 98 77
Astrological Energy: Stimulating
Color: Crimson

July

Mon 13

Tues 14
Jupiter at Opposition.

Weds 15

Thurs 16

July

Fri 17

Sat 18

Sun 19

Notes

Lucky Numbers: 82, 42, 66, 87, 42, 58
Astrological Energy: Inventive
Color: Ruby

July

Mon 20

New Moon in Cancer. 17:33 UTC
Saturn at Opposition.

Tues 21

Weds 22

Mercury at Greatest Western Elongation.

Thurs 23

July

Fri 24

Sat 25

Sun 26

Notes

Lucky Numbers: 31, 46, 25, 23, 43, 37
Astrological Energy: Methodical
Color: Peach

July/August

Mon 27

First Quarter Moon in Scorpio. 12.32 UTC

Tues 28

Delta Aquarids Meteor Shower. July 12th – Aug 23rd. Peaks night of July 28th.

Weds 29

Thurs 30

July/August

Fri 31

Sat 1
Lammas/Lughnasadh

Sun 2

Notes
Lucky Numbers: 35, 1, 7, 53, 26, 51
Astrological Energy: Constructive
Color: Lavender

August

Mon 3

Full Moon in Aquarius. Sturgeon Moon. 15:59 UTC

Tue 4

Wed 5

Thurs 6

August

Fri 7

Sat 8

Sun 9

Notes

Lucky Numbers: 30, 76, 90, 8, 41, 21
Astrological Energy: Independent
Color: Scarlet

August

Mon 10

Tues 11
Last Quarter Moon in Taurus. 16.45 UTC.

Weds 12
Perseids Meteor Shower. July 17th to August 24th. Peaks night of Aug 12th.

Thurs 13
Venus at Greatest Western Elongation.

August

Fri 14

Sat 15

Sun 16

Notes

Lucky Numbers: 65, 36, 98, 86, 47, 9
Astrological Energy: Aware
Color: Bronze

August

Mon 17

Tues 18

Weds 19
New Moon in Leo. 2:41 UTC

Thurs 20
Islamic New Year

August

Fri 21

Sat 22

Sun 23

Notes

Lucky Numbers: 40, 33, 63, 37, 45, 56
Astrological Energy: Spirited
Color: Mint

August

Mon 24

Tues 25

First Quarter Moon in Scorpio. 17.58 UTC

Weds 26

Thurs 27

August

Fri 28

Sat 29

Sun 30

Notes

Lucky Numbers: 22, 1, 30, 25, 2, 6
Astrological Energy: Enchanting
Color: Turquoise

August/September

Mon 31

Tues 1

Weds 2

Full Moon in Pisces. Full Corn Moon. 5:22 UTC

Thurs 3

September

Fri 4

Sat 5

Sun 6

Notes

Lucky Numbers: 86, 69, 78, 50, 71, 80
Astrological Energy: Unique
Color: Topaz

September

Mon 7
Labor Day

Tues 8

Weds 9

Thurs 10
Last Quarter Moon in Gemini. 9.26 UTC

September

Fri 11
Neptune at Opposition.

Sat 12

Sun 13

Notes
Lucky Numbers: 10, 12, 38, 62, 13, 91
Astrological Energy: Magnetic
Color: Coral

September

Mon 14

Tues 15

Weds 16

Thurs 17
New Moon in Virgo. 11:00 UTC

September

Fri 18

Rosh Hashanah (begins at sunset)

Sat 19

Sun 20

Rosh Hashanah (ends at sunset)

Notes

Lucky Numbers: 1, 54, 36, 80, 79, 57
Astrological Energy: Open
Color: White

September

Mon 21
International Day of Peace

Tues 22
Mabon/Fall Equinox. 13:31 UTC

Weds 23

Thurs 24
First Quarter Moon in Capricorn. 1.55 UTC

September

Fri 25

Sat 26

Sun 27
Yom Kippur (begins at sunset)

Notes
Lucky Numbers: 53, 89, 92, 97, 79, 71
Astrological Energy: Magical
Color: Maroon

September/October

Mon 28
Yom Kippur (ends at sunset)

Tues 29

Weds 30

Thurs 1
Full Moon in Aries. Harvest Moon. 21:05 UTC
Mercury at Greatest Eastern Elongation.

October

Fri 2
Sukkot (begins at sunset)

Sat 3

Sun 4

Notes
Lucky Numbers: 42, 11, 26, 5, 82, 14
Astrological Energy: Empathic
Color: Dark Orange

October

Mon 5

Tues 6

Weds 7

Draconids Meteor Shower. Oct 6th-10th. Peak night of Oct 7th.

Thurs 8

October

Fri 9
Sukkot (ends at sunset)

Sat 10
Last Quarter Moon in Cancer. 0.39 UTC

Sun 11

Notes
Lucky Numbers: 64, 1, 59, 48, 36, 61
Astrological Energy: Organized
Color: Chocolate

October

Mon 12

Columbus Day
Thanksgiving Day (Canada)
Indigenous People's Day

Tues 13

Mercury Retrograde begins.

Weds 14

Thurs 15

October

Fri 16
New Moon in Libra. 19:31 UTC

Sat 17

Sun 18

Notes
Lucky Numbers: 49, 37, 22, 78, 8, 4
Astrological Energy: Perceptive
Color: Salmon

October

Mon 19

Tues 20

Weds 21

Orionids Meteor Shower. Oct 2nd - Nov 7th. Peaks night of Nov 21st.

Thurs 22

October

Fri 23

First Quarter Moon in Capricorn. 13.23 UTC

Sat 24

Sun 25

Notes

Lucky Numbers: 96, 91, 20, 27, 33, 76
Astrological Energy: Mysterious
Color: Black

October

Mon 26

Tues 27

Weds 28

Thurs 29

October/November

Fri 30

Sat 31
Full Moon, Blue Moon in Taurus. Hunters Moon. 14:49 UTC
Uranus at Opposition.
Samhain/Halloween.

Sun 1
All Saints' Day

Notes
Lucky Numbers: 50, 44, 49, 97, 25, 1
Astrological Energy: Psychic
Color: Midnight

November

Mon 2

Tues 3
Mercury Retrograde ends.

Weds 4
Taurids Meteor Shower. Sept 7th - Dec 10th. Peaks on Nov 4th.

Thurs 5

November

Fri 6

Sat 7

Sun 8

Last Quarter Moon in Leo. 13.46 UTC

Notes

Lucky Numbers: 43, 18, 73, 51, 54, 92
Astrological Energy: Profound
Color: Royal Blue

November

Mon 9

Tues 10

Weds 11
Remembrance Day (Canada)
Veterans Day

Thurs 12

November

Fri 13

Sat 14

Sun 15
New Moon in Scorpio. 5:07 UTC

Notes
Lucky Numbers: 10, 7, 54, 57, 91, 21
Astrological Energy: Hectic
Color: Teal

November

Mon 16

Tues 17

Leonids Meteor Shower. Nov 6th-30th. Peaks night of Nov 17th.

Weds 18

Thurs 19

November

Fri 20

Sat 21

Sun 22

First Quarter Moon in Pisces. 4.45 UTC

Notes

Lucky Numbers: 75, 92, 5, 47, 99, 93
Astrological Energy: Structured
Color: Sky Blue

November

Mon 23

Tues 24

Weds 25

Thurs 26
Thanksgiving Day (US)

November

Fri 27

Sat 28

Sun 29

Notes

Lucky Numbers: 7, 25, 52, 75, 67, 55
Astrological Energy: Social
Color: Magenta

November/December

Mon 30

Full Moon in Gemini. Beaver Moon. 9:30 UTC
Penumbral Lunar Eclipse.

Tues 1

Weds 2

Thurs 3

December

Fri 4

Sat 5

Sun 6

Notes

Lucky Numbers: 87, 3, 92, 14, 83, 13
Astrological Energy: Impulsive
Color: Midnight Blue

December

Mon 7

Tues 8
Last Quarter Moon in Virgo. 0.37 UTC

Weds 9

Thurs 10
Hanukkah (begins at sunset)

December

Fri 11

Sat 12

Sun 13

Geminids Meteor Shower. Dec 7th-17th. Peaks nights of Dec 13th-15th.

Notes

Lucky Numbers: 67, 10, 7, 43, 76, 99
Astrological Energy: Vibrant
Color: Snow

December

Mon 14

New Moon in Sagittarius. 16:17 UTC

Tues 15

Weds 16

Thurs 17

December

Fri 18
Hanukkah (ends at sunset)

Sat 19

Sun 20

Notes
Lucky Numbers: 16, 85, 10, 96, 67, 1
Astrological Energy: Festive
Color: Powder Blue

December

Mon 21

Ursids Meteor Shower. Dec 17th – 25th. Peaks night of Dec 21st.
Great Conjunction of Jupiter and Saturn.
Yule/ Winter Solstice. 10:02 UTC
First Quarter Moon in Pisces. 23.41 UTC

Tues 22

Weds 23

Thurs 24

December

Fri 25
Christmas Day

Sat 26
Boxing Day (Canada & Uk)
Kwanzaa begins

Sun 27

Notes
Lucky Numbers: 33, 6, 30, 17, 80, 76
Astrological Energy: Graceful
Color: White

December

Mon 28

Tues 29

Weds 30

Full Moon in Cancer. Cold Moon. 3:28 UTC

Thurs 31

New Year's Eve

January

Fri 1
New Year's Day
Kwanzaa ends

Sat 2

Sun 3

Notes
Lucky Numbers: 23, 15, 12, 29, 71, 86
Astrological Energy: Aware
Color: Green Yellow

May the stars shine brightly in your world in 2020, and beyond.

About Crystal Sky

Crystal is passionate about the universe, helping others, and personal development. Crystal produces a range of astrologically minded diaries to celebrate the universal forces which affect us all. All reviews are read and appreciated.

Other Titles in the 2020 range:

Fairy Moon Diary 2020: Fairy Messages & Astrological Datebook
Shaman Moon Diary 2020: Shamanic Messages & Astrological Datebook

When not writing about the stars, you can find Crystal under them, gazing up at the abundance that surrounds us all, with her dog by her side.

www.ingramcontent.com/pod-product-compliance
Lightning Source LLC
Chambersburg PA
CBHW051801040426
42446CB00007B/468